The Enneagram Master

THE ROAD TO SELF-DISCOVERY, PERSONAL GROWTH AND HEALTHY RELATIONSHIPS; COMPLETE WITH A PRACTICAL 9 ENNEAGRAM PERSONALITY TYPES GUIDE

by Anne Brennan

TABLE OF CONTENTS

INTRODUCTION

Thank you for buying **"The Enneagram Master"**!

In the following chapters we will take a deep dive into the history, the meaning and the way to apply the Enneagram to your life. You will learn all about the nine personality types associated with the Enneagram system and how to understand and interact with each one. Every single person has a type, and you will learn how to find out which type you are, as well as tips and trick for cooperating and coordinating with others who fall into different Enneagram types. There are also certain factors like *wings* and *instinctual subtypes* that have a strong effect on your Enneagram types and you'll learn all about yours.

My final goal is that you – my reader – would have a chance to dig deeper into your personality and truly understand what makes you tick according to the Enneagram model. I'm positive that it will ultimately help you understand yourself better and have a deeper insight into your life and your place in this world.

Becoming the Enneagram Master requires processing a lot of information. The great news is that all this work has been already done "behind the screen", so the pages of this book will present you only with the most important and practical bits of information. My goal was to break down all of the crucial info that you need to know and present it in an easily digestible, easy to understand way.

I hope that this book will help you fully comprehend the nuance and complexity of the Enneagram system and you would be able to fully and completely apply your newfound knowledge into your life.

With much love,
Anne Brennan

CHAPTER 1

WHAT IS THE ENNEAGRAM SYSTEM?

Everyone has a personality. For a certainty, some people seem to have more of a personality than others, but even a low-key or subtle personality is nevertheless a type of personality. No two people are the same, but many people share certain personality traits or characteristics. Even two very different people might share a personality trait, maybe even a number of them, and they still may not seem very similar to each other at all. While a different set of two people might have many very similar personality traits and still seem like two wildly different people.

This is all part of the grand mystery of the human psyche. But science and psychology have come a long way in understanding what makes us tick and have been able to make sense of many of the more enigmatic aspects of the human mind. One such major development that scientist and psychologists have made in recent years is a system by which to classify, define and organize different personality types. The personality types form an interconnected figure that allows us to thoroughly understand how each type is affected and interacts with the others in the system. This figure is called **Enneagram**, and that is what we are going to discuss thoroughly in this book. We are going to go deep into the heart of Enneagram, its history, and what it means for you. So, please, ensure that your mind is receptive to learning and greater understanding as we dive into this fascinating story. Because if you allow it to, the Enneagram system can have a deep and profound positive effect on every aspect of your life.

The **Enneagram System**, or the **Enneagram of Personality**, is a model for the human psyche and is represented by *nine personality types* that are all interconnected. Each of the nine personality times, which are known as **Enneatypes**, are represented graphically on a geometric figure that itself is called the **Enneagram** (see below).

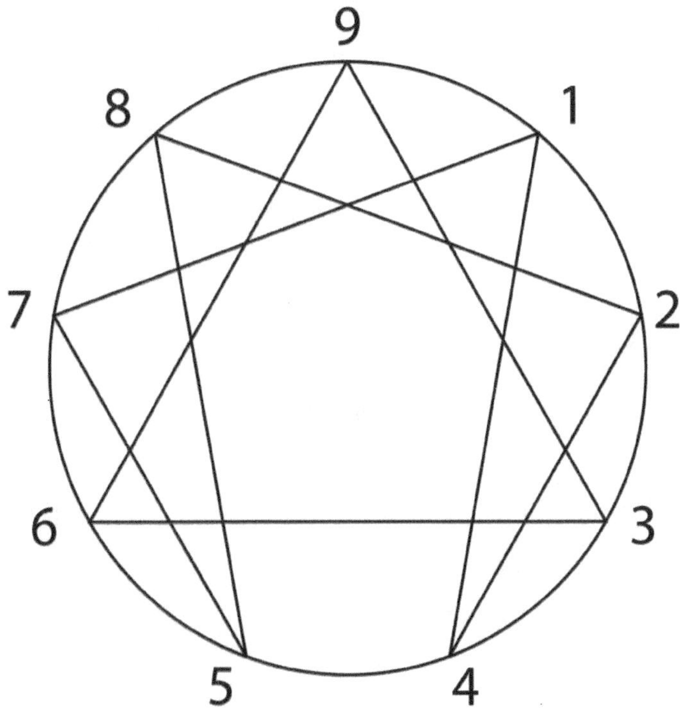

It's important to note that the Enneagram not only demonstrates the nine different Enneatypes but the *relationships between each one of them*. Understanding the key takeaways from each of the Enneatypes and their relationships to each other is the primary purpose of this book. We are going to take the time to learn about each one of them, what you need to know about how to discover *your own* Enneatype, and what that means for interacting with other Enneatypes. Understanding these definitions and relationships will become a very important part of your personal development in terms of self-acceptance, self-development, and self-awareness.

The word Enneagram itself has *Ancient Greek* roots.

- *Ennea*, the prefix of the word, derives from the Ancient Greek word for the *number nine.*

ἐννέα

- While the suffix *Gram* can refer to a model, or a system of points, or simply a drawn or written image that conveys information visually. The Enneagram system is all of those things.

γράμμα

While the specific roots and origins of the Enneagram and the system associated with it are long, meandering, and somewhat disputed, it is clear that the system goes back a *long, long time*, back into the era of oral and spiritual traditions. From the early days of philosophy and mathematics. It has been hypothesized that the Enneagram system dates back all the way to early *Pythagorean geometry* and the mathematics of the mystical.

Early Greek philosopher Plotinus speaks of human nature being a manifestation of nine different divine qualities. This he wrote in his book, which was called the Enneads.

It is also highly likely that the Enneagram system at some point in history found its way into the more esoteric aspects of *ancient Judaism*, probably introduced by the philosopher *Philo*.

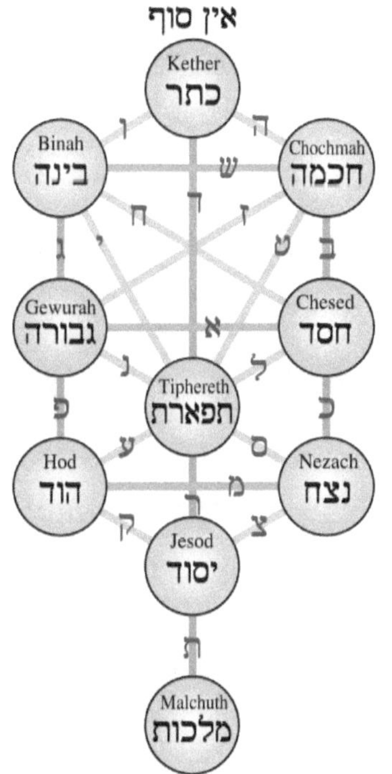

Eventually, the core concept of the Enneagram became embedded into the very branches of the *Tree of Life*, which is associated with the esoteric branch of Jewish mysticism known as the *Kabbalah*. The word Kabbalah itself can be translated as *"Nine-Foldedness"*.

There are also variations on the Enneagram symbol, similar enough to be certain of having the same, if not similar origins, appear in the traditions of some branches of the *Sufi* belief system, specifically in reference to a sub-organization called the *Naqshbandi Order*, which translates to the *Brotherhood of the Bees.*

And then on through the Middle Ages, we have evidence of the Enneagram system making its way into certain *Christian* beliefs and traditions. In fact, it's believed by some that the Enneagram was adopted and adapted in Christianity sometime during the medieval era, and eventually evolved or was adapted into the famous seven deadly sins from the Bible.

Furthermore, during the late medieval era, a Franciscan mystic by the name of Ramon Llull adopted nine principles into his philosophical and theological teachings as a way of integrating different traditions of faith and belief into the Christian tradition. Ramon Llull  published Ars Brevis (*Brief System*) in 1307, where we can observe a similar to Enneagram figure. In that figure the nine points present nine vices surrounded in a circle.

Another notable appearance of the Enneagram can be traced to the 17th century. A Jesuit mathematician from Germany by the name of *Athanasius Kircher* included an Enneagram depiction in one of his many religious texts (*Arithmologia*). In that work we can find a figure which is composed of three equilateral triangles.

Until recently, the Enneagram symbol and the philosophy behind it were relatively unknown in the Western world. The person who popularized the Enneagram in the early 20th century was *George Ivanovich Gurdjieff*. He was an adventurer, a mystic, a philosopher who devoted his life searching for the secret key to human nature.

The personality of Gurdjieff remains an enigma till this very day. There are conflicting opinions about his teachings. While some see in Gurdjieff a spiritual teacher, others consider him nothing more than a charlatan. Since this aura of mysticism concerning his ideas was a conscious decision on his side, little is

known how and where exactly he discovered the Enneagram. However it's through his work that the Enneagram became popular in Europe around 1910-1920s. Being presented at group lectures in Russia right before the Bolshevik Revolution, the Enneagram model and the Gurdjieff teachings started to spread throughout the rest of Europe and later in the rest of the world.

From all of this, we see a long, deep and often esoteric history of the Enneagram and its system. In modern times, the system has been adapted to modern philosophies and spiritual structures, but the origins of the Enneagram model make it clear to us that this is a system that has been used to understand human nature and our role in the spiritual world for *many generations and hundreds of years*. We today have the privilege of being a part of an ancient tradition that has guided and informed our ancestors through some of the most epic and important eras in history.

By learning about the Enneagram system and applying it to our lives, we are not only taking part in an ancient and noble tradition, but we are also taking advantage of thousands of years of research, knowledge, and expertise, both scientific and mystic, in order to bring greater self-awareness, self-understanding and self-growth into our lives.

9
8
1
7
2
6
3
5
4

CHAPTER 2

THE ENNEAGRAM TYPES

Now that we have had an introduction to the history of the Enneagram and a brief look into its origins and how widespread it is, we will now take an in-depth analysis into the nine Enneatypes that make up the Enneagram, and how the system works as a whole.

The Enneagram itself is the visual representation of the nine *Enneatypes*. Every single person is considered to have a *single dominant Enneatype*. Other types can influence someone's personality, which we will examine in much greater detail when we discuss *Wings* and *Instinctual Subtypes*, but each of the nine Enneatypes is something akin to a category, and every individual falls into one of them.

One question which often gets debated is whether an individual's Enneatype is determined prior or after to birth. The reality is that there's no consensus in the scientific and spiritual communities about this matter. From one hand an Enneatype may be determined *prior* to birth (implying a genetic pre-determination). From another hand it may be something acquired in early life – through learning and experience. This, of course, by and large is the great Nature vs Nurture debate, and the Enneagram system is no stranger to it. However, for our purposes here in this book, the determination of one's Enneatype is not important. What is important though, is knowing the *nature* and *differences* of the nine types, *how to interact* with each, and *how to determine which type we are*. This is what we will spend the next several sections on.

There is also another important aspect of understanding the Enneatypes. While it can be very important to understand which type we are, and how to identify Enneatype characteristics in other people, it's also very important to remember that *everyone is different*, and anyone can have *similarities and differences* from others. Two people with different Enneatypes may have almost *as many things in common* as two people of the *same type*. With this I would like to state that knowing someone else's Enneatype should **never** be a reason to pre-judge or stereotype others. In fact, there's **never** a good reason to pre-judge or stereotype others. And which Enneatype someone belongs to is never ever a determination of whether someone is a good person or a bad person. Only *getting to know* someone can tell you that.

On the other hand, learning about your own Enneatype can be one of the best and most important ways to understand more about yourself, and what you can do to excel and develop, as an individual, as a partner, or as a member of a team. The best way to identify which type you are (and that is what I advice!) is to simply read each of the following sections and take note of which Enneatype you identify with most. Please, be honest with yourself when assessing which type you are, as misaligning yourself with the incorrect Enneatype may do far more harm to your personal growth and development than good.

Alternatively, if you would like a more immediate result – there are many "complete" solutions out there which can test your closeness to each Enneatype. These tests vary in terms of their length and perceived depth of uncovering your Enneatype. Just to name a few: *The Essential Enneagram Test by David Daniels, The Wagner Enneagram Personality Style Scales by Jerome P. Wagner, The Riso-Hudson Enneagram Type Indicator by Don Riso and Russ Hudson.*

There are also many short personality tests out there, which promise to identify your Enneatype literally in 5-7 minutes (for instance, *enneagramtest.net*). However, as I mentioned above my recommendation would be to start with learning about the Enneatypes first and only then try to define which Enneatype you may belong to. This will help you avoid "locking" yourself into a particular Enneatype due to a very fast and potentially unreliable "quick" online Enneagram test.

Finally, remember too that each of the following Enneatypes, one through nine, are always associated with their corresponding number. That's why, when referring to various Enneatypes, I will be also using numbers as the Enneatype indicator.

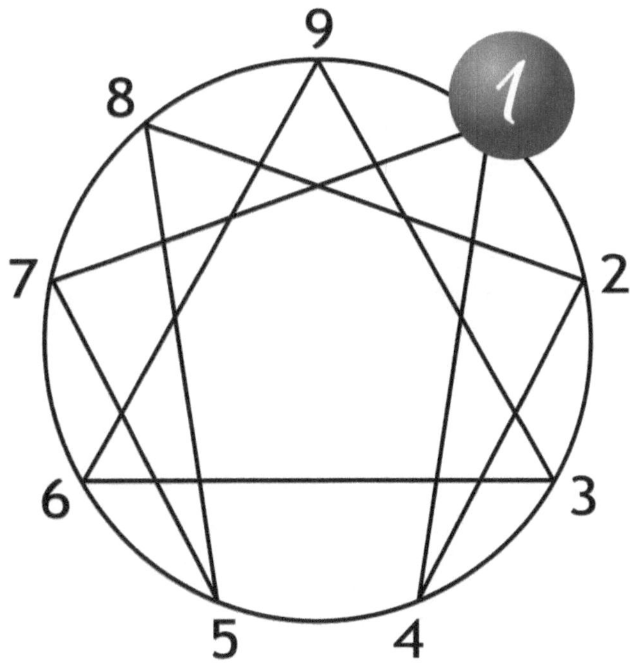

ENNEAGRAM TYPE 1: THE REFORMER

The *Reformer* is a perfectionist. Someone who is very responsible, and intensely fixated on improvement, whether personal or of the things around them. Essentially, these are people who are always striving to make everything better. A Reformer may give off the impression that nothing is ever quite good enough. Everything could always be just that much better.

Such tendency gives them a reputation of being a perfectionist, or some might even say an idealist—someone who is ever seeking to bring order to the chaotic world around them, someone who wants to improve, someone who wants to, well, reform.

Reformers have a very keen eye for detail. They tend to be acutely aware of the flaws that they possess within themselves, hence the constant desire for self-improvement. At the same time, they tend to also be very quick to see flaws in other people as well as in the various situations that they may find themselves in.

The constant pressure of what feels to them like inadequacies or flaws is what fuels their ever-raging zeal for improvement. This, of course, can be a great benefit to themselves and others, as their drive for perfection can help carry others who may be falling behind, but Reformers must always be aware of the effect of their drive for perfection on those around them. And as for those non-Type One's who regularly interact with Reformers it is very important to remember that their perfectionism isn't directed at you, but rather at a situation or scenario.

A Type One may have trouble always achieve what they see to be perfection, and therefore One's have a strong tendency to be very hard on themselves, and feel highly inadequate, feeling as though they have always fallen short. While they tend to always strive for improvement, they also tend to only see what they have not accomplished, rather than appreciating what they have. This often has the effect of causing Reformers to be frequently angry, as anger is all too often a byproduct of guilt and misplaced resentment. While a Reformer will often be very hard on themselves and often quite angry with themselves, they can also direct their anger at others for not meeting up to their standards, or to the world in general for being such a cesspool of imperfection (in their eyes, of course, whether it's true or not is up for debate).

It's important to note however, that anger is a negative quality, and due to the Reformer's nature as a perfectionist, they will quite often think of anger as a quality that must be repressed or eliminated. So while a One may deal with anger issues, that does not mean that they will be an outwardly angry person, but rather they may have deep internal anger at themselves. Thus it is important to treat One's with empathy and understanding, being aware that they may be suffering internally.

Finally, if you are a Reformer, remember to *take a break* once in a while! One's are often workaholics who never quit until they get the job done.

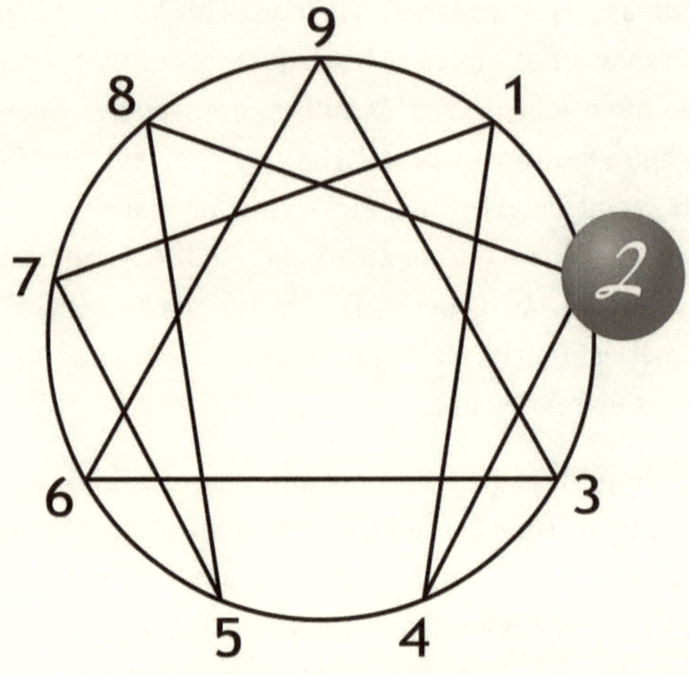

ENNEAGRAM TYPE 2: THE HELPER

A person with the personality type of the *Helper* is exactly what they sound like, a helper. A person who wants to help others, and feel that they need to be needed.

Helper's generate their own self-worth from helping others. Their deepest held value is being there for those who need it. Their most lofty ideal is that of love, and their most honorable duty is that of selflessness. In a Two's eyes, the entire purpose for existence is to *give to others*. Helpers tend to be very active and involved in their community. They also tend to be highly aware socially. A Two is generally very extroverted and sociable. They will never forget your birthday, or anyone else's. And they will almost always go above and beyond to be there in a pinch for a friend, partner, or team member.

Helper's tend to be very in tune with their emotions, and they are certainly not afraid of their emotions. They are warm and caring people can care very much about all of their personal relationships, whether friendly, romantic, or otherwise. They tend to devote a great percentage of their time and energy to their relationships, but they also often expect to be recognized and appreciated by those individuals in those relationships for the efforts that they put into them.

A lot of a Helper's personal identity and self-worth are frequently derived from what they perceive to be their level of ability to help others. In order for them to feel good, they need their loved ones to feel good. They feel important when a loved one comes to them for help, guidance or advice. Virtue and selflessness are things that make a Helper feel complete and whole.

If you identify as a Helper, you must be very cautious of your own needs, and make sure that you are not neglecting yourself in favor of helping others. Constantly being available for others can be very exhausting, and it can lead to emotional issues such as poorly controlled mood swings, and can even have physical effects. It is not uncommon for Helpers to simply burn out. Self-care is <u>vitally</u> important for Helpers. It is crucial for them to understand that it is virtually impossible for someone to completely be available to others if they are not taking care of themselves and ensure a healthy balanced life, emotionally and physically.

For those with loved ones who are Helpers, the most important thing to remember is to give back. You must not take advantage of a Helper's nature. That is their primary vulnerability and to exploit it would be the lowest form of malice. You can help Helpers by accepting their help and acknowledging their assistance. Never forget to remind them of how much you need them and how much you appreciate their help and support. Ultimately, a Helper is all about support, so just make sure that you are supporting the supporter as much as you can, and everyone will be better.

Helpers are some of the most special and delicate souls around, and they can't do what they're made to do without the rest of us allowing them to.

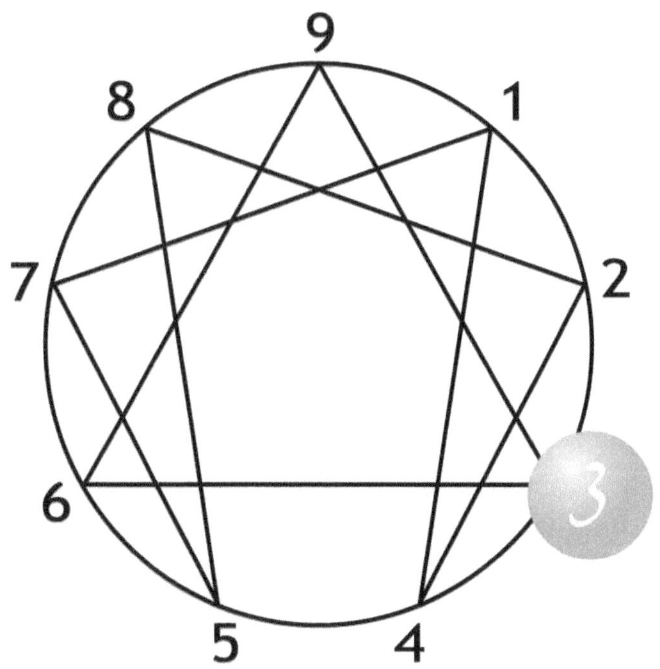

ENNEAGRAM TYPE 3: THE ACHIEVER

The third Enneagram type is that of the *Achiever*. Achievers are people who are highly attuned to the presentation of success. They frequently strive to attain validation in their lives and actions.

A major aspect of the lives of Type Threes is the need to *feel validated for them to feel worthy*. An Achiever wants to be admired, they need to succeed. Threes are often very hard working individuals, and they also tend to be extremely competitive, and intensely focused on the pursuit of their goals. These are people who are relentless in their pursuit of success. Nothing is good enough unless it's the best. A successful career doesn't mean anything unless they are at the top of their firm, for example. Or being attractive isn't good enough unless they are more attractive than everyone else.

Achievers often think of themselves as being self-made, regardless of how accurate that assessment actually is. It is very common for a Three to find a field of expertise or area of practice that they do in fact excel at, as without the validation they receive from excelling in that particular field, they would have a very difficult time indeed. Their need for validation via success and achievement is so complete that it may even come across as desperate.

Achievers tend to be very extroverted, socially competent and in many cases undeniably charismatic. They have an ability to present themselves to appear the way they want to, and they are usually very self-confident and highly driven. Their practicality may border on pragmatism, and may even go as far as being ethically questionable. However, Threes also tend to be very energetic, and their excitement and energy can often rub off on others they associate with. In fact, the concept of "friends" and "associates" can be somewhat blurred for Achievers as their zeal and charisma tend to make them excellent networkers and employees, able to take advantage of the way people respond to them in order to advance themselves in their careers, or socially.

Achievers should be very careful with confusing real happiness, with the kind of false happiness that is dangled like a carrot in front of them by our culture and the constructs of our society. It is crucial that a Three look inward and discover what real success means to them. While society may tell you that wealth and a strikingly attractive partner are what success is, that may not be what you actually need in your life to feel fulfilled. If you are an Achiever, get in tune with what really makes you happy, and make that the target of your goals.

Intimacy is often very challenging for Threes. The deep-seated need for validation can be very detrimental to an Achievers' self-image, regardless of how they present themselves, and it can be very easy for them to be internally overwhelmed with shame and fear. If you have a loved one who is a Three, make sure you always bear in mind what they may be feeling inside, even if they are not always forthcoming about it, and make sure to help them see what real success really is.

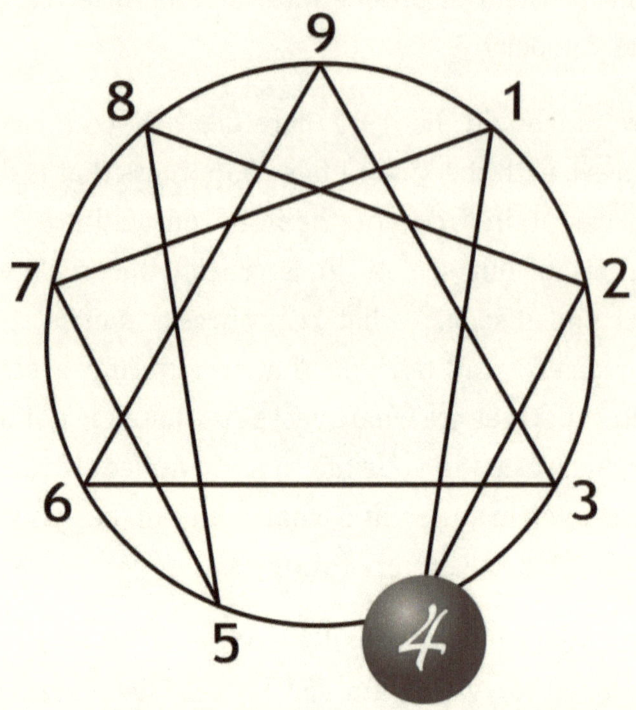

ENNEAGRAM TYPE 4: THE INDIVIDUALIST

The *Individualist* is a person who feels somehow different or unique. Quite often, this may be due to a Four's feeling of a lack of true identify, resulting in identity seeking behavior.

Fours are often people who tend to construct their personal identity around the idea of being in some way *outside of the mainstream*; as being some kind of a fringe element. They are not just people who conduct themselves in an individualistic way, they are people who are actively and self-consciously individualistic.

Self-perception can certainly vary of Individualist to Individualist, but they may often see their individuality as either a gift or a curse; and quite often a combination of both. The idea of being outside of regular society, set apart from the common masses, is highly appealing to a Four, but such a personality can also lead Individualists to feel that they are missing out on the fun and social comfort of the 'commoners' that they so desire to be apart from.

This often confusing set of conflicting feelings can lead to a Four feeling like they are in some ways better, or superior, to the common population, while at the same time secretly feeling envious of others, or simply like they just *don't belong*. Fours are sometimes plagued with feelings of wanting to fit in with others, but at the same time harboring a deep fear that achieving increased social acceptance will somehow diminish their individuality, the quality they hold most dear. These mixed and conflicting feelings can be quite painful for the Individualist and may be associated with intense feelings of shame and fear.

Individualists tend to be very sensitive emotionally, as well as being not just emotionally deep, but emotionally complex. There is a lot of internal conflict in Fours. They often see being misunderstood and ignored as part of their identity and something to protect, while at the same time feeling unappreciated and undervalued for the exact same reasons. Individualists often come across as being temperamental or moody, and it is not at all uncommon for a Four to simply retreat from the world when they are faced with circumstances they feel they can't handle.

Fours tend also to be very internal in nature, whether intellectual or emotionally inclined, they tend to internalize things and be highly reflective. Much of an Individualist's frustrations may come from a feeling of not being able to express or articulate the things they feel inside, and thus, Fours are very often inclined toward the arts. And even if a Four doesn't pursue the arts, they frequently tend to have a good appreciation for art and often feel that they have excellent taste.

If you have an Individualist loved one, the most important thing to remember is to *listen* and to encourage them to *always express themselves*. It is very easy for an Individualist to fall into the trap of fantasizing about better conditions rather than acting, so try to encourage a Four's loved one to action.

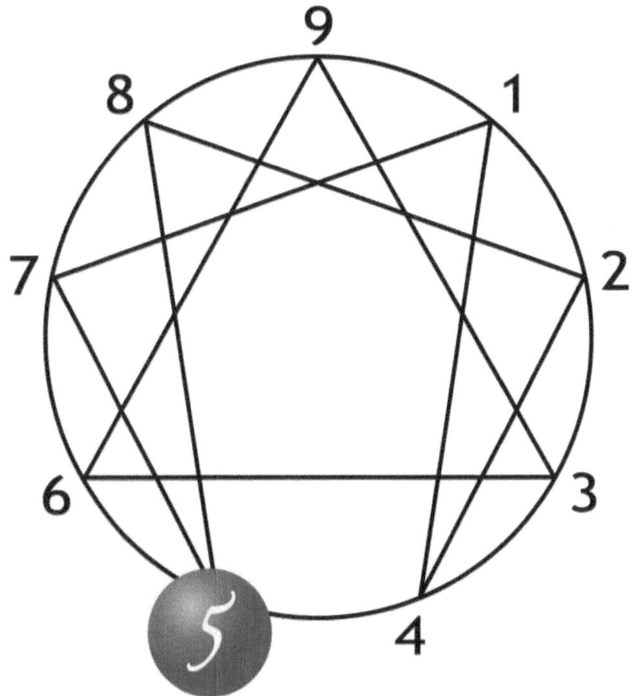

ENNEAGRAM TYPE 5: THE INVESTIGATOR

Investigators are people who spend a lot of time thinking. They tend to stand at a figurative distance and observe. They tend to feel as if they do not possess the inner strength necessary to face their life, and as a result they have a tendency to withdraw into themselves, and to retreat to the perceived safety of their mind, where they can prenpare themselves mentally for all of the challenges the world can offer up to them.

Fives are very comfortable with their thoughts and feel at home in the realm of their minds. They are almost always highly intelligent. Investigators tend to read quite a lot and often eschew fiction and entertainment that they may consider being either beneath them or a distraction that takes them away from learning or improving their mind. Fives are also generally very thoughtful people and enjoy engaging in deep, meaningful conversation when in situations in which they feel comfortable.

An Investigator's interests often lie in science, but it's equally likely that a Five may find themselves interested in the arts and in the humanities. In any case, it is highly likely that a Five will find an area of particular interest and become an expert in that field.

It is certainly not uncommon for Fives to be a little bit on the eccentric side. They don't very often feel any need or desire to alter their worldview in order to align with the majority. They can be a little bit like the Individualist in that regard.

An issue that Fives often have, however, is that while they have a high level of comfort within their own thoughts, they are rarely as comfortable in public or in a social setting. As a result, it is common for Fives to have a hard time dealing with and expressing their emotions. They may also find it hard to meet the needs of a partner in a relationship. Generally speaking, Fives have a tendency to be very shy individuals, who are so non-intrusive and non-confrontational that they even have a hard time asking for help, even if they have a loved one who would be more than willing to do so.

Investigators often take on a persona of aloofness or of intellectual arrogance. This is generally for the purpose of compensating for feelings of inadequacy or not feeling properly equipped to deal with the world, but as a result, this often leads to distant interpersonal relationships and a lack of real intimacy in their lives. However, it is worth it to work through this with Fives, as once they become comfortable with someone, they can often be counted on as a great companion and life-long friend.

Investigators should strive to be open with their emotions and with others. It may be hard to trust others, but once someone earns that trust, deep, meaningful and truly important relationships can come from it.

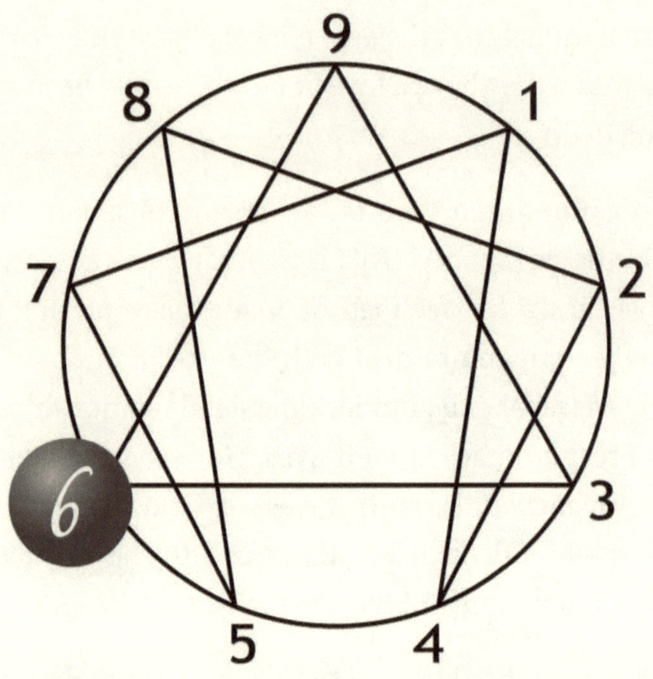

ENNEAGRAM TYPE 6: THE LOYALIST

The personality of a *Loyalist* can be boiled down to one thing: *a conflict between trust and mistrust*. A frequent feeling of Sixes is insecurity. They often feel like they never really have steady footing. In short, a person with the Type Six personality is someone who is largely controlled by fear and anxiety.

The anxiety that a Six experiences may have any number of root causes, and as such can be very difficult to thoroughly describe or define, but the general quality that Sixes tend to have in common is a personality in which fear plays a major role and tends to sit front and center in their hearts and minds. These fears can manifest in the form of a generally worrying type of attitude, and Sixes also have a tendency to constantly think about, almost fantasize about, all of the things that could go wrong in any given scenario.

While this tendency certainly does have its advantages — Loyalists make excellent troubleshooters, for example — it also has the effect of depriving Sixes of the peace of mind that they often so desperately need, and they also tend to lack spontaneity, as any unknown or unfamiliar act or action is met with a flood of negative, intrusive thoughts regarding the safety or success of said act or action.

This type of anxiety and fear is what is often referred to as 'defensive suspiciousness' and it is rooted in the Loyalist's feelings of being poorly equipped to defend against the many challenges and dangers the world could potentially throw at us. This, naturally, results in a personality that is very slow to trust, but on the flip side, once that trust is earned and achieved, it is nearly unshakable. Even that though can have a downside, and a Loyalist may end up extending their trust far beyond what has been actually earned.

Loyalists often just feel like they need someone or something to believe in. Thus, Sixes can frequently have a strange relationship with authority. While their distrusting nature often will lead them to reject or even actively distrust authority, they can also somewhat counterintuitively tend to be drawn toward external sources of authority, whether that be spiritual, individual or political. While a Six is generally more likely to reject institutions like religions, law enforcement, or governments, they may be inclined to fall into smaller, insidious organizations that are designed to pray on people like them and others.

In either case, Loyalists are generally not actively aware that their actions and intentions are often driven by fear, and it could be very helpful for them or their loved ones to examine that and help find that understanding. Anxiety and fear can be a constant presence for Sixes, which means that it is very possible that they have no idea how anxiety is affecting their everyday choices and decisions. The loved ones of Sixes can help immensely by working through their anxieties with them and helping them see that their actions are often reactive to their background anxiety rather than being autonomous choices.

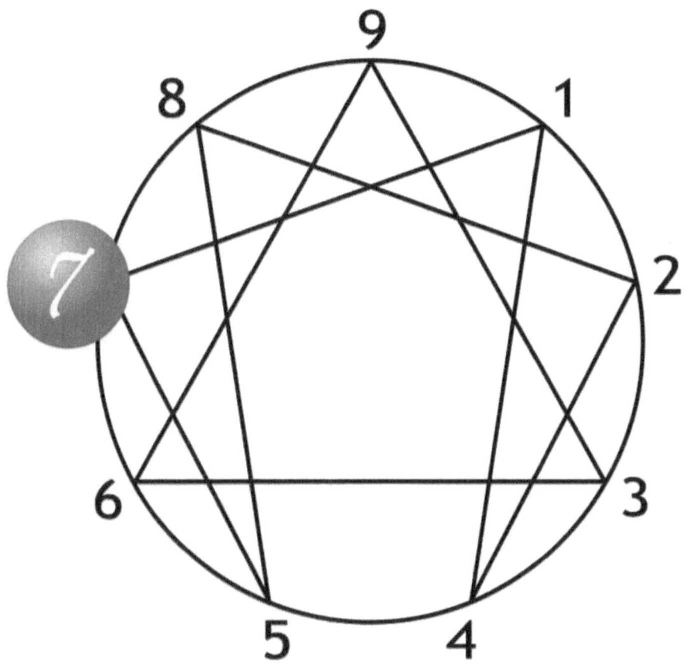

ENNEAGRAM TYPE 7: THE ENTHUSIAST

Enthusiasts tend to be well planned, pleasure seekers, who seem to be always looking for a distraction.

Sevens are the type of person who is always very concerned about doing things, taking action, having fun, living an adventure. They tend to be very forward thinking and focus on their future. They tend to be rather restless and often feel as though the next big thing is just around the corner. They also tend to be very quick thinking, love making all of the plans for themselves and others, and generally have lots and lots of energy. Enthusiasts are creative and open-minded, they tend to have lots of talents, and naturally, they are generally very much extroverted. The enthusiasm from which their name is derived manifests in the form of never believing in any kind of self-denial, and enjoying every sensual pleasure the world has to offer.

Enthusiasts are generally very practical and highly skilled people. They are often very good at self-promotion, self-marketing and working a crowd to get what they want. It is not at all uncommon for an Enthusiast to have an entrepreneurial passion, and they can generally drum up as much enthusiasm among others for a project, plan or endeavor. Enthusiasts tend to be most successful when they are afforded the opportunity to hone their skills and focus on a particular talent. However, having said that, focusing on one thing in particular is not always an easy task for an Enthusiast. An attitude of always waiting for the 'next big thing' can have the effect of diluting a Seven's efforts and dividing their attention from the task at hand.

One of the biggest potential problems for an Enthusiast is that they often pursue pleasure as a compulsion. It can be an overpowering force, rather than a well-executed plan. Sevens also tend to be afraid of negative thoughts and states of mind, which can be pushed away by always filling up their attention with distractions. As such, Enthusiasts are very often multi-taskers who are always inclined to keep their options open, and by constantly seeking stimulation. Because of this tendency, Enthusiasts must be very careful, as they are highly prone to addiction, whether it's substance abuse, shopping, gambling, or sexual in nature.

Sevens often tend to hold themselves in a relatively high esteem, and highly value their own talents. You'll often find an Enthusiast playing down their shortcomings and frequent vices in favor of their strengths and good qualities. They may also have strong feelings of entitlement and have a tendency toward being self-centered and egotistical. Because of the fact that Sevens very frequently avoid confronting their darker and more painful emotions, it's not uncommon for them to be poor empathizers, never truly acknowledging or understanding the suffering and pain of others.

It's important to always encourage a Seven's creativity. This will help Enthusiasts stay focused on their natural optimistic qualities, making them feel satisfied and fulfilled, which will naturally positively affect those who surround them.

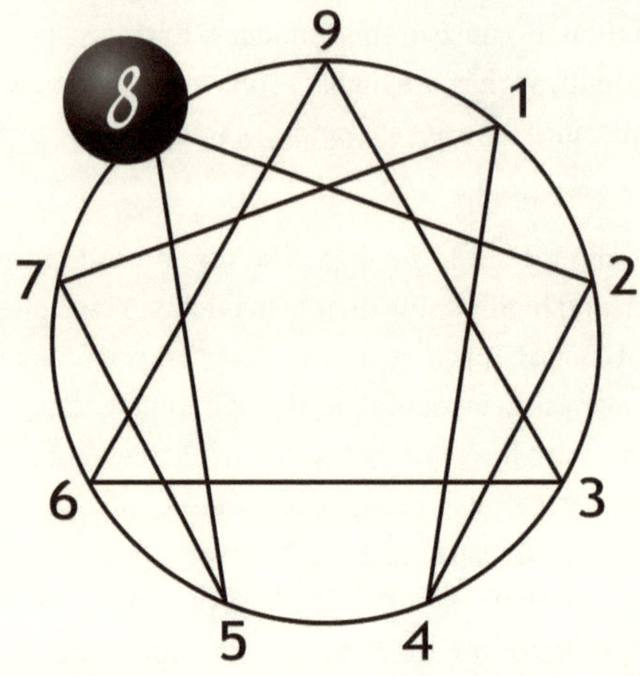

ENNEAGRAM TYPE 8: THE CHALLENGER

An Eight is a person who takes charge of a situation. Their compulsion to lead is less about controlling people, and more about a deep-seated aversion to being controlled by others.

Challengers are just what they sound like. They challenge authority, they cannot tolerate being controlled. And it's not just control by people they have an aversion to; a Challenger can no more abide being controlled by circumstance than they can by a person. A Challenge is the master of their own destiny; the only person who can determine their own fate.

An Eight may at times veer somewhat toward the more domineering aspect of their Ennea, as the most sensible way of avoiding all control, at least in the eyes of the Challenger, is to assert control over others. To a Challenger, the only way to truly and completely escape control is to exert control over everyone and everything. And while this tendency, in some cases an urge or even compulsion, can quickly spiral into serious conflict and problems, it should not be assumed that every Challenger is an overpowering, domineering individual. In many cases, an Eight simply understands their nature and why they experience the needs they feel, and they exercise them in a healthy way. For example, when a Challenger recognizes that the needs and desire of their personality type have the potential to be harmful, even dangerous, they will often choose to exert their control over their own urges, keeping them in check. Those tendencies, however, will always remain there, just under the surface. So if an Eight wishes to retain control over their own urges, they must be ever-vigilant.

On the positive side, Challengers generally have very good and strong instincts, and they are usually quite well equipped mentally and emotionally, to set and follow their own path. They intend to get what they want out of life, which is as much as possible, and they have no problem acting on their intentions. Eights are fiercely independent, financially, spiritually, and ideologically, and they shun what they consider to be *'herd mentality'* at all cost. They never fall for populist lies, and they would never trust authority. They often may think of themselves as something of an outlaw, if not literally, then at least metaphorically.

Challengers also tend to exhibit very intense physical appetites, as well as being far less likely to experience guilt or shame, and therefore must be very deliberate about empathizing with others when satisfying their needs. Closely associated with these issues is a Challenger's general aversion to vulnerability, making intimate relationships difficult for them.

Challengers are usually healthiest mentally when they have made peace with the society in which they live. Whether that's achieving financial independence or home out in a rural area, a Challenger can find peace when they make peace with the world they live in and the people they love. When a Challenger finds this peace they will understand what true independence is.

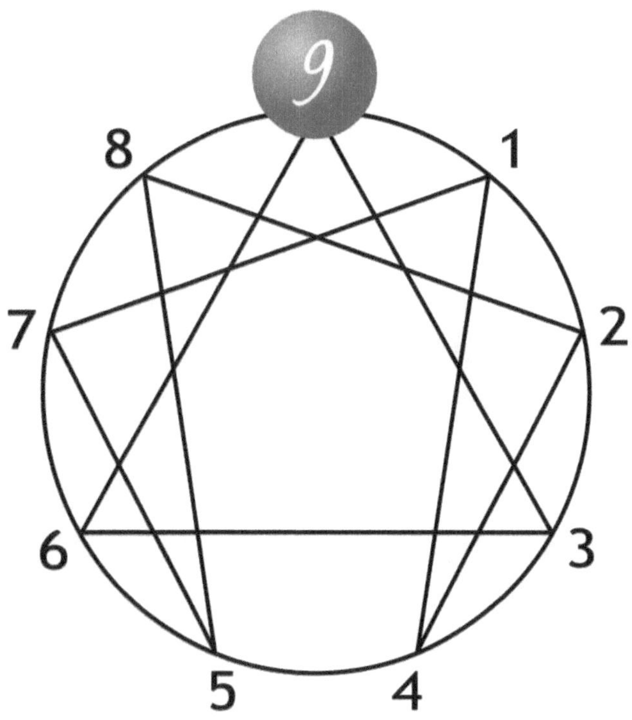

ENNEAGRAM TYPE 9: THE PEACEMAKER

In the eyes of a Nine, their mission in life is to maintain peace and harmony and engender unity for all. *Peacemakers* avoid conflict if at all possible. It is very common for Peacemakers to be introverts, as in their view, the world is full of nothing but conflict, and the more you interact with it, the more opportunities for conflict arise. This may often lead to Nines being somewhat withdrawn and reclusive.

There certainly are Peacemakers who have very active and healthy social lives, but in all likelihood, those social interactions are psychically and mentally exhausting, and they will generally need to spend some time alone to 'recover', so to speak. However, contrary to popular wisdom, Nines are not generally anxious or stress-prone people. In fact, they tend to be rather easy going. After all, going with the figurative flow generates a good deal less conflict than challenging and questioning things. Nines tend to be very likable as they seek to make people happy and not rub anyone the wrong way. As humor is a great tension breaker, you'll often find that Peacemakers are also the ones who are quickest to crack a joke.

Peacemakers tend to be very trusting people. They see the best in others, they want the best for everyone, and they often truly believe in their hearts that everything will work out well. They are very optimistic people who always keep a positive attitude and worldview.

Nines can often exhibit an aversion to change. Change can feel like a form of conflict to a Peacemaker, so it can be very difficult for them to tolerate and accept. A Peacemaker often requires a figurative *even keel* in their life to feel comfortable and secure, and change is a major disruption to that stability. It is very important that Peacemakers do not fall into the trap of being unable to generate any motivation to take any action in their lives, and as a result become stagnant, unable to affect any positive change in their lives.

The irony here is that by the Nine's very nature, they are generally highly adaptable and very much capable of change. It's the motivation to change and acceptance of change that is challenging for the Peacemaker. Thus for those with loved ones who are Peacemakers, it's important to remember to *encourage and support* them to *accept the changes* that they need to. Remind them of times in the past when positive results came from change, and how easy it was in retrospect. This will help bolster the Peacemakers confidence to make the changes they need to make.

The biggest thing that Peacemakers tend to be guilty of is not giving themselves the credit they deserve. So remember to *commend and recognize* the good qualities and positive achievements of the Peacemakers, and remind them that you appreciate them. And if you are a Nine, reflect on what you have accomplished and how far you've come. You may surprise yourself.

CHAPTER 3

WINGS AND INSTINCTUAL VARIANTS

Now that we've broken down what all nine personality types in the Enneagram are, you may feel like you fully understand which type you are, and how to proceed from here. Or you may be feeling even more confused. You may have identified with more than one type or saw aspects of yourself in a few of them.

Well, that's why we're going to talk about some of the factors that can *modify* you base Enneatype. Understanding *Wings* and *Instinctual Variants* will help you more thoroughly understand your own personality type.

WINGS

Most prominent Enneagram experts and theorists subscribe to and teach the notion that an individual's personality is influenced and altered by one or both of the Enneatypes adjacent to their own. Hence the concept of 'Wings', as in, the personality type on the wings of the primary personality type. So if you are a Seven, your Wing might be Six, Eight, or a little of both.

It may be possible that you very clearly and solely identify with one type. That's fine. It's very unusual for someone to be *completely and only* represented by one Enneatype, but most people have one *core* type. The Wing, however, can be thought of as the *second* aspect of your personality, or the *second side* of it. If you truly want to come to a full understanding of yourself and your relationship to others, you will want to have a full understanding of Wing and which Wing of your dominant type modifies your personality.

Most people are thought to be primarily influenced by *one* wing, although technically, by the very nature of the system, each person possess elements of both of their wings. For the most part, though, each individual has their own dominant type, and then one particularly influential wing. It is also possible to be equally defined by two adjacent Enneatypes. This is known as having *'balanced wings'* and while it is not particularly common, it is certainly not unheard of.

Many people claim to experience the development or awakening of a 'second wing' as they grow older. It has been thought that this is part of the natural aging and developing process. It has also been theorized that as a person ages, they simply collect more and more experiences, attain more wisdom, and achieve a more balanced understanding. In that regard, it is certainly possible that rather than truly becoming a different Enneatype or developing a new wing, these older individuals may simply have the experience and wisdom to empathize and understand other Enneatypes that are not intrinsically their own.

But Wings are not the only Ennea modifier. Next, we'll learn about our *natural instincts*, how they are classified, and what they mean about us.

INSTINCTUAL SUBTYPES

Enneatypes help us define the primary attributes that guide our everyday behavior, but every one of us at times acts or reacts on instinct. How does that affect our personality type? Does instinct play a larger role in determining the nature of our personality?

Well, the short answer is *yes*, our instincts do play an important role in defining our personality type. But it's not as complicated as it may seem. Essentially, we can categorize instinct into three different subtypes that we refer to as *Instinctual Subtypes*. Each of the nine Enneatypes can be modified by each of the *three Instinctual Subtypes*, making for a total of *twenty-seven* different personality subtypes represented by the Enneagram.

The first subtype is the ***Self-Preservation Subtype***, in which those with this natural instinct variant usually will strive to seek out independence and comfort. People with this subtype will generally give the most attention in their lives to the thing that brings them well-being. They will likely be highly focused on their health, or perhaps their home, or quite possibly their finances. In fact, it's not at all uncommon for those with this subtype to be highly focused on all of the above. They will generally tend to crave interpersonal contact somewhat less than others. Not to say those don't enjoy it, they simply don't have the same need as others. Often, Self-Preservation people will be less emotionally open than others and may come across as less spontaneous or easy-going.

The next Instinctual Subtype is the ***Social Subtype***. These are people who are in their element when they are functioning in a group or as a team. They operate well in a group and tend to be helpful, cooperative and team-oriented. This can be a very positive element to bring to a group, as when a problem arises, a Social Variant will be quick to bring the group together to solve the problem as a team. However, Social Variants should be careful to check their ambition, as their natural instinct to work in a group often turns into a need to lead a team, which of course is healthy and positive — every team needs a leader, after all — but they should nevertheless be careful not to become too overbearing or domineering.

Finally, we have the ***Sexual Variant***, sometimes called the ***One-to-One Variant***. It's important to note that a Sexual Variant's instincts are not always about sex, but that certainly plays a frequent and important role. A Sexual Variant is someone who craves one on one intimacy and this need is often pursued sexually. As you may image, Sexual Subtypes tend to be the most passionate of the three Subtypes, and they tend to have lots of energy but may be a little bit on the emotionally volatile side. Being in a relationship is often a major priority for Sexual Variants, but they must be always wary to only enter into healthy relationships. Generally speaking, Sexual Subtypes tend to be relatively quick to conflict and may tend to be less interested in traditional rules and responsibilities.

CHAPTER 4

APPLYING WHAT YOU'VE LEARNED

The major advantage of knowing your own Enneatype is understanding how you should be interacting with other Types. Below you may find a helpful and concise guide. Please, remember that this is a very practical overview of potential interactions between the Enneatypes. If you wish to dive into the details behind each of these relationships, there are many good resources out there which can satisfy your curiosity. One good place to start is visit "The Enneagram Institute" (www.enneagraminstitute.com).

So let's get on with our relationships guide!

TYPE ONE RELATIONSHIPS

❶ When a One interacts with another One, it may seem like that could be disastrous, but it can actually work out quite well considering how well their ideal align. However, Ones should be careful about getting into a never-ending improvement project.

❷ A One matched with a Two may be quite complementary as well. A Reformer and a Helper tend to fill in each other's gaps quite well.

❸ A One pair with a Three has the potential to be a very productive and idealistic relationship. Just be sure you are devoting as much energy inward as you are outward.

❹ A relationship between a One and a Four can be a very free, easy-going and expressive one. Caution should be in order though, as a Four's tendency to act on emotion and feeling may clash with your logical reasoning.

❺ Ones tend to also have a lot in common with Fives, with the primary difference being that Fives tend to have a strong focus on the abstract, while Ones are more practical. Therefore both should remember to remain open-minded to each other's ideas.

❻ Even more similar, Ones and Sixes are so alike, they often misidentify as each other. Sixes may be a little bit quicker to emotion though, so One should remember to be patient.

❼ Sevens are arguably the most complementary to Ones, in an "opposites attract" kind of way. While they balance each other out very well, a One must be aware that a Seven's idealism and free-spiritedness may at times come across as childish or undisciplined.

❽ Eights potentially can be somewhat likeminded with Ones, with each being likely to be passionate about truth and justice. However, their differences tend to chip away at the relationship, so beware.

❾ And when it comes to Nines, Ones tend to understand them very well, despite differences, and a Nine often has a tempering effect on a One. However, different approaches to stress and conflict may lead to imbalance.

TYPE TWO RELATIONSHIPS

❶ Twos should value Ones for their complementary qualities, and similar goals and values. But be sure to keep the lines of communication open to avoid conflict.

❷ A Two paired with another Two, obviously will be a warm and caring relationship. However, jealousy can very easily creep into such a pairing, even if it's a friendship or familial relationship.

❸ Twos and Threes are both highly emotional, even though that's more apparent in Twos. However, what at first may appear to be common goals, may turn into points of serious stress and contention.

❹ A Two and a Four may struggle to achieve intimacy at first, but once they do, it will be warm and passionate. Unspoken wants and misunderstood needs may make this pairing more appropriate friendship, although when it works, this can make for a very healthy romantic pairing.

❺ Twos and Fives are certainly opposites, in terms of both thoughts and feelings. This can lead to intense attraction between them, and it can work rather well. Just be careful to have well-defined boundaries and strong communication.

❻ Twos and Sixes tend to have very loyal and serious relationships. This can make for a strong foundation, but make sure to remember to bring joy and levity into the relationship.

❼ Sevens on the surface may seem quite similar to Twos, and they are both certainly friendly, outgoing, sociable people. Differing long-term ideals and feelings of lack of space may lead to trouble though, so beware to keep communication free and open.

❽ Twos and Eights don't seem very similar at all on the surface, but they can both have similar interiors. However, be aware and respectful of differing values.

❾ Nines are helpers and nurturers just like Twos. However, this often leads to a relationship in which no one takes charge.

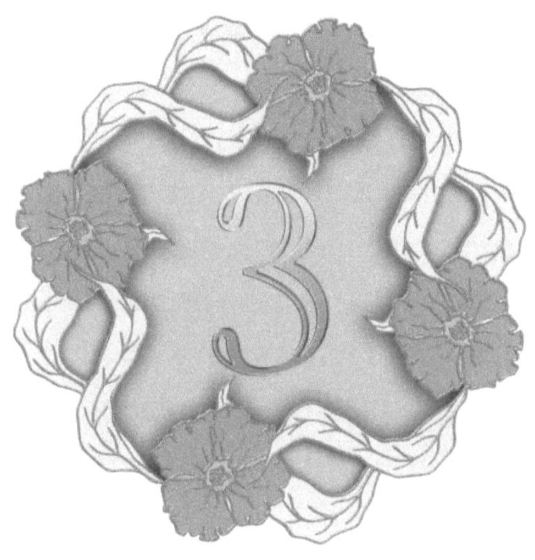

TYPE THREE RELATIONSHIPS

❶ A Three paired with a One is a very goal-oriented relationship, with only One-One or a Three-Three pairs being more so. Be careful of blind spots that may develop while you both have your eyes on the prize.

❷ Three's and Two's can be a very fulfilling pairing. Three's should be aware that a Two's helpfulness may come across as possessiveness.

❹ Fours tend to possess a number of qualities that Threes lack, and vice versa, so they make good compliments. But be careful of mutual low self-esteem dragging you down into a spiral of negativity.

❺ Fives can bring a creative spark to a Three that may have been lacking otherwise, and you can expect to be seen as a very intelligent and successful relationship, although a mutual desire for excellence may lead to undue criticism of perceived weaknesses.

❻ A Six paired with a Three is one we don't see terribly often, even though it may seem to make sense. It certainly can work, just be aware that you may end up possessing many of the same negative qualities.

❼ A particularly complementary pairing, Threes and Seven's each bring their own energy to very similar qualities. But having that much energy and intensity in one pair could lead to a powder keg of volatility, so be sure to communicate through any potential issues.

❽ Three and Eights are both the types of people who know what they want and will work hard to get it, so they can make for a very effective and goal-oriented pair. This is also the type of pair that could be prone to jealousy and competitiveness, so both will need to be able to handle that.

❾ A Nine paired with a Three makes for a relatively common pair. Nines are supportive and encouraging, which can be very powerful in enhancing a Threes positive intrinsic qualities. Be careful with this pairing, however, to not become too entrenched in routines and the dopamine loop of positive feedback.

TYPE FOUR RELATIONSHIPS

❶ Fours and Ones both can have a strong desire to create and build things, literally or figuratively. Both believe in self-expression and tend to be idealistic. But if those ideals aren't very closely aligned, they can find themselves drifting away from one another before too long.

❷ A Four and Two pair will be very open and emotionally supportive, with both parties being warm and passionate. Because the tendencies of each partner though, be careful not to develop an unhealthy pattern of the Four needing to have constant problems for the Two to fix.

❸ Fours generally tend to match rather well with Threes. They have complementary attributes that can keep that pair productive and healthy. It is possible though, for this pairing to develop issues of requiring each other's validation in too many, if not all areas.

❹ Despite the moniker of Individualist, two Fours can make quite a good pair; each understands the other's desire for individuality. Be careful that the relationship doesn't become too self-serving though, which each half generally knowing exactly what they what to get out of a relationship.

❺ Fours and Fives make for deep, complex pairings that can be very fulfilling. It's possible for an intimacy-independence imbalance to develop, though.

❻ A Four and a Six tend to be naturally, if maybe superficially attracted to one another. Be sure to have a strong foundation before getting too deep.

❼ Fours and Sevens make for a dynamic, 'opposites attract' type of pairing, and the introvert coupled with an extrovert is a relatively common and successful partnership. Each half will need to be actively seeking to grow and learn from one another.

❽ A Four matched with an Eight is sure to be a highly creative coupling. But with each partner having a penchant for being larger-than-life, beware of it quickly becoming more than you bargained for.

❾ Nines and Fours can both be highly compassionate and empathetic, while also being quick and private. As long as there each half respects the other's privacy, this can be a very successful partnership.

TYPE FIVE RELATIONSHIPS

❶ A Five and a One tend to have a number of similarities; they are both intellectual and a little bit emotionally private. But while both types tend to be very fact-oriented, their individual ideas of what a fact is and how to arrive there can cause conflict.

❷ Fives and Twos aren't the most common of pairings but when they do happen they tend to be highly complementary, given their opposite nature. While that can be fitting for some, it can lead to emotional imbalances where not all needs are always mutually met.

❸ Another relatively opposite pairing, Fives and Threes are actually fairly common. Often it can be something of a creator-muse type of relationship, which can be highly rewarding, but also potentially dangerous, if one or both come to only be able to derive self-worth from the other.

❹ Fives should be open to, but cautious of pairing up with Fours. Fours can certainly help Fives stay in touch with their emotions and feelings, but this type of relationship can become demanding for both.

❺ Double Fives are an interesting combination. At least on the surface, another Five seems like a perfect fight for a Five, and that can be true, but beware that this relationship will be prone to over-analyzing and intellectualized over emotional.

❻ Fives and Sixes both tend to have a primarily mental focus in life. This is often a type of relationship that starts as a friendship and becomes something more. Maintain open-mindedness for success.

❼ Fives and Sevens both tend to have a lot of mental and intellectual energy. This can be positive and healthy for both. Be sure to address stress and conflict with care and patience.

❽ Eights can be very complementary to a Five, and Fives can learn a lot of Eights. Power dynamics can play an ugly role if not careful though.

❾ A Five paired with a Nine will be a good environment for emotional and personal space. A Five should seek out if a quiet, unobtrusive relationship is appealing; if not, fun away!

TYPE SIX RELATIONSHIPS

❶ Type Sixes should be aware that type Ones often misidentify as Sixes because they are so similar. This can lead to heavy judgment and criticism, so be aware.

❷ Sixes and Twos tend to be very responsible and supportive toward each other. A control dynamic could quickly present itself though.

❸ Threes don't pair very often with Sixes, but when it works, it really works. Be prepared to put in a lot of time and energy to keep it healthy and stable.

❹ Fours tend to be drawn to Sixes, so they may well come to you. You'll likely feel like kindred spirits, but mutual fixations of abandonment issues can lead to emotional troubles.

❺ Fives can bring some healthy critical thinking into a relationship with a Six, but you'll both have very different ways of thinking, so make sure to make communication and trust a priority.

❻ A Six paired with another Six can make a strong couple. They tend to have a deep understanding of one another, which can make for a strong, trusting relationship. Don't let too much negativity enter the relationship though, as emotions will deteriorate quickly.

❼ Another highly mental pairing, Sevens can bring a good deal of healthy stimulation to a Six. They can bring much joy and happiness into a relationship. However, a Six may perceive a Seven to be too unstable and unpredictable, so self-awareness and honesty are key.

❽ A Six and Eight have the ability to create a very strong, healthy, long-term relationship. It will be highly supportive, deep and solid. However, both types can have a tendency to conceal emotions and weaknesses, so openness and complete trust are very important.

❾ A very common and healthy relationship, Sixes and Nines tend to be stable and highly secure. Each type provides what the other needs. But there is such a thing as too much of a good thing, so be careful not to get too comfortable with the relationship or it could quickly become stagnant and cease to grow and develop.

TYPE SEVEN RELATIONSHIPS

❶ Ones can bring a lot of good habits and attention to detail into a relationship with a Seven, which can be very important in a Seven's life. But on the flip side, if there isn't strong teamwork and cooperation, the One may begin to perceive the Seven as being undisciplined and immature.

❷ A Two paired with a Seven is a generally fun, outgoing and high-energy relationship. A Two will bring in some emotional depth that a Seven may lack, but the Seven may begin to feel suffocated and held back after a while.

❸ Another high-quality pairing, a Three will be very compatible with a Seven in terms of energy levels and tendency to be outgoing. Three may bring a level of sensitivity to the relationship, but the constant high energy may lead to emotional burnout.

❹ Four can bring a lot to a Seven in terms of focus and in getting in touch with their feelings. Fours and Sevens tend to have a high degree of early attraction, which could lead to immediate sparks, but strongly aligned interests and pursuits are important if that level of interest is to be maintained.

❺ Sevens and Fives tend to make good reciprocal pairings. Fives can bring a degree of self-reliance and independence to a Seven, for whom those things may not be a priority, however, under stress, Fives may tend to detach emotionally, so the Seven must be aware of this.

❻ Sixes can have a strong reinforcing effect in a relationship with a Seven. They tend to compliment a Seven's ability to think outside the box with concrete steps and plans. However, beware of developing conflicting goals.

❼ A relationship formed from a double Seven pairing can be spotted from a mile away. Very high energy, fun and spontaneous, and always the entertainers. However, the potential trouble spots are just as easy to see; a relationship primarily characterized by wish-fulfillment and throwing caution to the wind can become unhealthily hedonistic in a hurry.

❽ An Eight and Seven pairing tend to be very strong-willed and assertive. It can also be very practical and thoughtful, but if either partner doesn't have a healthy outlet for their energies, it could become a big problem.

⑨ Sevens paired with Nines are one of the more common pairings seen. They can both be very positive and optimistic, with Nines bringing a particularly calming, steadying nature to the relationship. This pairing is often very successful and good at defusing problems, just be careful to be aware of what your partner isn't communicating.

TYPE EIGHT RELATIONSHIPS

❶ One's can be highly attracted to Eights, so keep an eye out. They will bring will and energy into the relationship, but cracks can begin to show after a while because of the opposite nature of the two.

❷ Twos have a lot in common with Eights. Expect a lot of passion and vitality in the relationship, but differences in interpersonal relationships could lead to problems.

❸ Eights and Three can work together quite nicely, and Eights nature can be quite comforting and supportive for a Three, but both partners must know their limits in order to not become over-worked, and bring stress into the relationship.

❹ Fours can be an excellent pair with an Eight if you're looking for a highly creative and stonily emotional connection. However, those emotional connections could become impassioned arguments if not careful.

❺ Eights and Fives generally make for really good pairs, with Fives helping Eights to be more empathetic and thoughtful. However, insecurity could play a strong role here, so be aware.

❻ Eights and Sixes tend to be a very strong and concrete pair. They tend to be quick to trust each other, but trust can backfire.

❽ Eights and Sevens make for strong, trail-blazing partners. But a high-energy, productive pair could become a trap for misplaced anger if not careful.

❽ The double Eight pair is one of energy and vitality. But it can also be highly volatile and ego can begin to play a role.

❾ Meanwhile, Nines tend to look up to Eights, which can be powerful in the short-term, but lead to unhealthy power imbalance in the long-term.

TYPE NINE RELATIONSHIPS

❶ Nines and Ones tend to be attracted to one another, but not always for the best. Each has very different ways of approaching problems, which can be a major issue if not handled correctly.

❷ Nines and Twos are often very similar in a lot of ways, with both being nurturing in nature. Communications breakdown can become a problem early on if not established early.

❸ A fairly common partnership, Threes tend to help Nines value themselves more fully. This generally is a positive and healthy thing, just be careful not to become complacent.

❹ Fours have a tendency to bring out more expressiveness of feelings in Nines. That's definitely a positive, just make sure not to become disengaged or distant.

❺ Fives often have the ability to draw an emotional connection out of Nines. But tensions can start to take hold early, so be prepared to address them, or let them go.

❻ Nines and Sixes make for a very firm and stable relationship, with Sixes bringing a certain inquisitiveness and mental element to the table. However, both partners must be comfortable speaking their minds and addressing concerns or else problems will fester under the surface.

❼ Nines paired with Sevens are very common, having a healthy combination of similar and complementary qualities. Sevens can bring a strong element of fun and a sense of adventure to the relationship. But while this can be a very happy and positive pair, be careful to not ignore the negative or pretend there are no issues, as that will only make them worse.

❽ Eights and Nines both tend to have strong leadership qualities. This can make for a focused, purposeful pair, or it can lead to the issue of each partner vying for supremacy, so cooler heads must prevail for this pair to succeed.

❾ And finally, a double Nine pairing is one of the more common double pairs, as a Nine is in fact quite well suited to support and encourage other Nines. This will be a very steady, stable pair, but that can be a double-edged sword, as anything, even external elements, that upsets that stability can be a major problem.

CONCLUSION

Thank you for completing **"The Enneagram Master"**! I sincerely hope that it was an interesting read and you answered all (or at least most) of the questions you had about the Enneagram system.

What is next? I think the next step is to continue to be in touch with the Enneagram and with your Enneatype. Now that you know *who* you are and what your type's *strengths and weaknesses* are, you will be well-equipped to venture into all of your interpersonal relationships with the full knowledge and understanding of the power and strength of the Enneagram.

In addition to the above, I would like to believe that no matter which type you are, or which type your loved ones are, the knowledge that you have acquired from this book will help strengthen bonds, enrich lives and dissuade conflict.

And there is no end to learning! The Enneagram has depth beyond what a book like this can reveal. If you're interested in learning more about the Enneagram, you can always dive deeper into its world to learn more about yourself and the people you care about. There is so much more to discover.

With much love,
Anne Brennan

www.ingramcontent.com/pod-product-compliance
Lightning Source LLC
Chambersburg PA
CBHW051223250726
48655CB00006B/2562